SCHOOL OF THE INCARNATION OF THE ONLY-BEGOTTEN

St. Cyril of Didouseya
Archbishop of Alexandria

Translated by: D.P. Curtin

INCARNATION OF THE ONLY-BEGOTTEN

Copyright @ 2021 Dalcassian Press

All rights reserved. No part of this publication may be reproduced, distributed, or transmitted in any form or by any means, including photocopying, recording, or other electronic or mechanical methods, without the prior written permission of the publisher, except in the case of brief quotations embodied in critical reviews and certain other non-commercial uses permitted by copyright law. For permission request, write to Dalcassian Press at dalcassianpublishing at gmail.com

ISBN: 979-8-3302-3451-6 (Paperback)

Library of Congress Control Number:
Author: Curtin, D.P. (1985-)

Printed by Ingram Content Group, 1 Ingram Blvd, La Vergne, Tennessee

First printing edition 2021.

INCARNATION OF THE ONLY-BEGOTTEN

INCARNATION OF THE ONLY BEGOTTEN

CHAPTER I. What is Christ? The name of Christ neither acquires the power of definition, nor does it signify any substance, such as it may be, as perhaps a man, or a horse, or an ox; but what is done in something has a greater significance: for some of the superiors were anointed with oil, according to what pleased God at that time, and the anointing was a sign of the kingdom to them. And the prophets were insensibly anointed with the Holy Spirit, so that from that also they were called Christs. Finally, the blessed David psalms from the person of God and says: Do not touch my christs, and do not malign my prophets (Ps. 14:15). And the prophet Habakkuk also said: You went out to save your people, to save your Christians (Heb. 3:13).

But in Christ, the Savior of all, we say that the anointing was indeed made: moreover, neither symbolic, as if made with oil, nor as if in prophetic grace; but not that which is meant to be done for the completion of any business of this kind, such as we say was done in Cyrus, king of the Persians and Medes. For he led an army against the Babylonians, at the instigation of Almighty God himself. For it has been said: These things the Lord says to my Christ Cyrus, whose right hand I took hold of (Is. 45:1). And that man, since he was a worshiper of idols, was named Christ, because he was, as it were, anointed to the kingdom, by a heavenly vote, and was ordered by God to attack Babylon violently.

But that is more about Christ. Because of Adam's transgression (Rom. 5:14) sin had reigned over all, and the spirit had departed from humanity (Gen. 6:3), and for that reason she was engaged in all evils; but it was necessary, that by God's mercy he should be restored to his former state, and that he should earn the Spirit: man became the only begotten Word of God, and with an earthly body he appeared to the earthly. He was also free from sin, so that both in him and in him alone, the nature of man, crowned with the praises of innocence, might be enriched by the Holy Spirit, and thus reformed to God through sanctification. For the grace begun by Christ, who is our firstborn, also passes to us; and teaching us this, the blessed David psalms to the Son: You loved justice and hated iniquity, therefore God your God anointed you with the oil of joy (Ps. 44:8).

The Son of Innocence was anointed with the praises of our example, and, as I said before, the nature of man enlightened in him, and already worthy to receive the Holy Spirit, would no longer depart, as before, but would rather remain in it. Therefore, it is written that the Spirit descended upon him and remained upon him (John 1:32). Christ is therefore said to be the Word of God, who was made for our sakes and a man like us, and in the form of a servant; but he anoints with his divine Spirit those who believe in him.

CHAPTER II. How should Emmanuel be understood? Emmanuel is called God the Word, who took hold of Abraham's seed, and in the same way as we have partaken of flesh and blood (Heb. 2:14). And Emmanuel is interpreted, God with us. But let us confess that the Word of God was with us, not locally: for in what place is not God who fills all things? Nor is it seen that he is present to us by reason of help; For it was said in this way to Jesus the son of Nave: And as I was with Moses, so I will be with you (Jos. 1:5). But what has happened in ours, that is, in humanity, has not abandoned its nature: for the nature of God's Word is unconvertible.

Moreover, why is it that, when it is plainly said to Jesus the son of Nave, that as I was with Moses, so I will be with you, is not Emmanuel named? Now the reason is the same: for even if it is said that he was with some of the saints; yet we do not say that the Word of God was made with us, except at the time when, according to what Baruch says, he was seen on earth, and conversed among men, and finding every way of instruction, and giving it to Jacob his child, and to Israel, whom he loved. for he is our God, and no other will be compared to him (Bar. 3:38).

For as far as the nature of God is concerned, he was not yet with us; for there is a great difference between divinity and humanity; and the difference of natures is too great.

And therefore, the divine David was calling to mystical proximity, God the Word, which had not yet come to us, saying in his spirit: Why, O Lord, have you gone far away (Ps. 10:1)? Therefore, he no longer departed, but was with us, who, when he had remained, seized the seed of Abraham, as I said; and he also took the form of a servant, and the sight of man is on the earth.

But Christ and Emmanuel designate the same son to us, partly because he was anointed in our manner, receiving the spirit of the human nature of man, as in himself and first. For the beginning of the race was set, again himself anointing, as God, with the Holy Spirit those who believe in him; she will give birth to a son, and his name will be called Emmanuel (Is. 7:14). For when the holy Virgin was indeed made pregnant by the Holy Spirit, she gave birth to a son according to the flesh; then also Emmanuel was said: for he was with us, through the carnal generation of the incorporeal; and that was what was signified by the voice of David. God will come manifestly, our God, and will not be silent (Ps. 49:3); and I think that: I who have spoken, am available. For the Word spoken by the prophets, as yet incorporeal, also came bodily.

CHAPTER III. What is Jesus? Indeed, by the power of intentions, by which it is necessary for us to call one Son of God, Christ, and Immanuel, and Jesus are the same; and that, as it were, the name was made from a thing: for he, he says, will save his people from their sins (Matr. 1:21). For as Emmanuel signified, that the Word of God was made with us throughout the generation from the woman; and Christ, because he became man, is said to be anointed next to us as a human: so also, Jesus, because he saved us his people, which most of all shows him, in truth and by nature, the Lord of all. For man is not said to be a common creature; but it is more fitting, to say all things, that he should be the only begotten, even though he was made man.

Perhaps someone will say: But the people of Israel were called Moses. To this we will say that the people of God were indeed named, and that was true. But since he was led astray, and made a calf in the wilderness, he was dishonored by God: for he no longer deigned to name his people, but he had already destined them for man. But not so with us: for we are our own children, inasmuch as God is, and by him all things were created. but we are the people of his pasture, and the sheep of his hand (Ps. 49:7). Finally, he also said of us: My sheep hear my voice and follow me (John 10:27). And again: I have other sheep, which are not of this fold, and I must gather them together, and there will be one flock and one shepherd. And he also commanded blessed Peter: Simon John, do you love me? Feed my lambs, feed my sheep (John 21:17).

CHAPTER IV. For this reason, man was called the Word of God. He is named man, since he is by nature God, the Word of God the Father: for in the same way as we are partakers of blood and flesh (Heb. 2:14). For in this way he appeared to the earthly, not losing what he was, but assuming the nature of humanity perfect in his nature. Nevertheless, God also remained in humanity, and is the Lord of all, as he who in nature and truth was born from God the Father. And the wisest Paul shows this to us most clearly: For the first, he says, was man from the earth out of the mire; the second from heaven (1 Cor. 15:45).

And the holy Virgin gave birth to a temple united to the Word; but it is said from heaven, and rightly so, Emmanuel: for from above, and from the substance of God and the Father, his Word was born. yet it is so also from above. And John testified, saying of him: He that cometh from above is above all (John 3:31). And Christ himself said to the Jewish people: You are below, I am above (John 8:23). And again: I am not of this world (John 14:16), although a part of the world is called man; but with this also he was above the world as God. For we remember clearly those who said: And no one ascends into heaven, except the Son of Man who descends from heaven (John 3:13). Now we say that the Son of Man descended from heaven, through dispensational unity, giving to the Word the glory of his own flesh and the brightness of his divine majesty.

CHAPTER V. For this reason, the Word of God is called empty. God the Word, full according to nature, and perfect in every respect, and distributing from his fullness the goods of his creatures, saying: I will pour out of my spirit upon all flesh (Isaiah 44:3). We say empty; nothing in its proper nature was violated, nor, as it were otherwise, changed, nor made inferior in any part: for it is also unconvertible and unchangeable, like its begetter, and was never capable of any passion. But when he became flesh, that is, man, he made his own poverty of humanity. First, that he once became man, though he remained God: secondly, that he took the form of a servant, who is free according to his nature, as the Son. And so, since he himself is the Lord of glory, he is said to receive glory; since he himself is life, he is said to be quickened, and takes power over all, since he himself is the king of all; since God is equal to the Father, he was obedient to the cross, and the rest. But when these measures of humanity meet, it leads to familiarity with the flesh, and fulfills the dispensation, remaining what it was.

CHAPTER VI. How Christ is one. The divine Paul writes: Although there are many gods and many lords in heaven and on earth; but to us there is one God the Father, from whom are all things, and we from him; and one Lord Jesus Christ, through whom are all things, and we through him (1 Cor. 28:5). But truly the wisest John said of God the Word, that all things were made by Him, and without Him nothing was made (John 1:3). And the blessed Gabriel preached to the holy Virgin, saying: Behold, you will conceive in your womb and give birth to a Son, and you will call his name Jesus (Matt. 1:26). When then, the divine Paul remembers that all things were made through Christ Jesus; but let him confirm the power of the sentence, and evangelize that God was the workman of all things, saying the true thing, the divine evangelist; and the angel's voice also pointed out that Jesus Christ was truly born of the Holy Virgin, and we do not understand God the Word without humanity. but we say one effect from both, and God made man, the same from the Father, as the Word, born divinely, and from the human woman, as man: not as if he were called according to the beginning of substance, when he is said to be born according to the flesh; but indeed he was born before all the ages, yet at the time when he should have fulfilled the dispensation, he was also born of a woman according to the flesh. Therefore, although others are called by a similar appellation of Christ, yet there is one through whom all things are, Jesus Christ; not that he became the workman of all things,] but that God the Word: through whom all things were made, in the same way as we are partakers of flesh and blood (Heb. 2, 14), and was called man, yet did not lose his being, which he was: for so it was in the flesh is understood to have become the workman of all by merit.

CHAPTER VII. How one is Emmanuel. In the last centuries, God the Word is said to have become man, and, as the divine Paul says, he was manifested through his sacrifice (Heb. 9:27). And what is the sacrifice? For he offered his body for us as an odor of sweetness to God and the Father, and he entered into the holy place once, not through the blood of goats or bulls, but through his own blood. For in this way he procured eternal forgiveness for those who believed in him (Eph. 5:2; Heb. 9:13). Therefore, there must indeed have been many saints before him; but none of them was named Emmanuel. Why? For the time had not yet come when he should be with us, that is, come into our nature through the flesh, he who is superior to all creatures. Therefore, one Emmanuel, for once he became a man, the only begotten, then when he was perpetuated by carnal generation through the holy Virgin. For it was said also to Jesus the son of Nave: I will be with you (Josh. 1:5). But that was not Emmanuel. It was also with Moses; but neither was he named Emmanuel. Therefore, whenever we hear that the name of the Son was given, God with us, let us wisely understand that he was not with us in the last times, as it is said that he was once with the saints: for he was only a helper to them; but he was with us, that is, he became like us, when he had not lost his nature: for he is unchangeable, like God.

CHAPTER VIII. How we lead the gathering. Reunion is accomplished in many ways: for some, separated by affection or will, and discordant with one another, are said to be united, by means of social reconciliation, deposited together. Again, we say that those things are brought together, whether they are brought together by other means, or by composition, or by mixture, or by tempering. And whenever we say that the Word of God is united to our nature, it seems that its method of union is superior to all human thought. For it was not by the above-written methods that secret union was made, and was thoroughly known to no one, except to him to whom all things are known.

And no wonder if we are overcome by this kind of thinking, when, inquiring into our affairs, how they are, we confess that the discovery is beyond the limits of our mind; and in what manner we think that the soul of man is united to his body. Who can express it? But if it is necessary for those who are used to scarcely understanding these little things; nay, and those who are able to understand, to conjecture things so subtle and transcending all reason: we say that it is fitting to think (though it is a smaller prayer to the truth) that the union of Emmanuel himself is such as one understands the soul of man to have to his body. For the soul considers all that is of the body to be its own, although by its own nature it is exposed to bodily and natural passions, and those which approach from without: for the body is moved by natural concupiscences, and the soul consents, and in no way may it participate, yet the result of concupiscence is its own pleasure leads And if by chance the body is struck with a sword, or tortured, she indeed sympathizes with the fact that her own body suffers: but she herself in her nature tolerates no torture at all.

However, above this too we say that there is a union which took place in Immanuel: for it was necessary for him to grieve the soul united with his body, so that while he was afraid of the passions, he submitted his neck to God. But of God the Word, it is wrong to say that we sympathize with passions: for God is impassive, and far unlike our things; but he was indeed united to the flesh, having a rational soul, by which he himself, being impassive, knew what befell the soul, and indeed, like God, crushed the infirmities of the flesh; yet he led them to be his own, as his own body. Therefore, it is said that he was hungry, that he was tired, that he suffered for us.

Therefore, the union of the Word, which is made with humanity, is not unreasonably compared to our things. For just as the body is of another nature apart from the soul, and yet one is made and called man from both, so also from the perfect subsistence of God the Word and from perfect humanity Christ is one, the same God and man at the same time. and indeed, God brings the Word to His own, as I said before, those things which are proper to the flesh, because it is His own body, not another's. And he makes common the operations of his divine majesty as with his own flesh, so that he might also give life to the dead and heal the sick.

CHAPTER IX. Of coal. But if it behooves the examples of the divine Scriptures to show, as it were by a figure, the union; Come on, let's say that we can. Blessed Isaiah, said he, one of the Seraphim was sent to me, and he had a coal in his hand, which he took with tongs from the altar, and he came to me, and touched my lips, and said to me: Behold, this touches your lips, and take away your iniquities. He will cleanse you and your sins (Isaiah 6:6). But we say that coal presents to us the figure and image of the Word made man: if it touches our lips, that is, if we have confessed faith in him, then it makes us pure from all sin, and frees us from our former crimes.

For the rest, as in the image, although he may behold the Word of God united to humanity in the coal, yet he has not thrown away what it had been.

But he transformed the assumed nature into his own glory and operation: for just as fire, attached to wood, and penetrating it, indeed embraces it, and although it does not cease to be wood, it nevertheless changes its power and appearance, and transfers all of itself into wood, and with it already as if any one thing were esteemed, understand the same about Christ. For God, having inestimably gathered humanity, indeed preserved it in what it had been, and He himself remained what it was; yet once united, as if he were already thought to be one with her, making the things that are hers his own; but he also imparting to him the operation of his own nature.

CHAPTER X. That the body of the incorporeal divinity has become flesh itself, having a rational soul: and that if we wish to separate it from itself, we shall doubtless undermine the dispensation which is understood in Christ. In the Song of Songs he is introduced to us, saying our Lord Jesus Christ: I am the flower of the field, and the lily of the valley (Can. 2:1). Just as, then, a smell is indeed an incorporeal thing, it has, as it were, a proper body, that in which it is; yet one of the two is understood to be a lily. But his reason is corrupted by the departure of one thing: for there is a smell in the subject's body. Thus also in Christ we understand the nature of the divinity, which disperses its most excellent majesty, like a most sweet fragrance, to the world, as if in a subject, being in the body of humanity; and that which is incorporeal by nature, by dispensational union, I may almost say was made corporeal; because he wanted to be known through his body, for in it he worked divine signs. Therefore, that which is incorporeal can be understood as in its own body, just as the fragrance is in the subject flower; yet the lily already smells and is called a flower.

CHAPTER XI. When God the Word was truly united to humanity, the substance [that is, of subsistence] remained unconfused. According to the will of God, the holy tabernacle was erected in the wilderness, and in it Emmanuel was formed in many ways. Almighty God said to the divine Moses: And make me an ark of the testimony of incorruptible wood, two cubits and a half long; and you shall gild it with pure gold, you shall gild it without and within (Ex. 25:10). But wood indeed, since it is incorruptible, is the figure of an incorruptible body: for the cedar is incorruptible; But gold, as if it were more precious than other materials, shows us the majesty of the divine substance.

Take heed therefore that the whole ark be gilded with pure gold without and within. God the Word had indeed been gathered in the holy flesh, and that is, as I think, that the ark was gilded on the outside. Indeed, that he also made the rational soul, which was part of the body, his own, is evident from this, that he also commanded that it should be gilded inside the ark. Now that the nature or substance remained unconfused, we know from this: for the gold superimposed on the wood remained what it was, and indeed the wood was adorned with the adornment of gold. yet it did not cease to be wood. But the fact that the ark is taken as an image of Christ can be made clear by several proofs. For he went before those who are from Israel, seeking rest for them. Christ also said somewhere: I will go and prepare a place for you (John 14:3).

CHAPTER XII. Since God was the Word, he became a man, and not simply a man, honored by bare conjunction, was called to equal dignity, or authority, to the God of the Word, as it seems to some. The divine Paul indeed says that the mystery of piety is great (1 Tim. 3:16). And truly this is how things are: for he was manifested in the flesh, since God is the Word; but he is justified in spirit. For in no way does he seem to be restrained by our infirmities, although he was made man next to us: for he committed no sin: and he appeared also to the angels. For they were not ignorant of his generation according to the flesh. and thus he was believed in the world. And the divine Paul proved it by writing thus: For this reason, remember that sometimes you Gentiles in the flesh, who cut off the foreskin, by what is called circumcision in the flesh, because you were at that time without Christ alienated from the conduct of Israel, and guests of the covenants, had no hope of the promise having and without God in this world (Ephesians 2:11). There were therefore nations in the world without God, when they were without Christ. But since nature and truth acknowledged him to be God, they too were acknowledged by him, confessing their faith, and he himself was taken up in glory, certainly divine. For the blessed David sings: God ascends in jubilation (Psalm 46:6). For he certainly ascended with a body, and not in a naked deity: for God was incarnate.

We believe, therefore, not in one like ourselves to a deity honored by grace, lest we be discovered to be the worshipers of man; but rather to the Lord, who appeared in the form of a servant, and who was truly like us, and yet God remained in humanity: for God the Word, having taken on flesh, did not put down what he was; It is understood, however, that God and man are the same at the same time.

And indeed, the reason of faith is thus, and rightly so. But if someone should perhaps say, what is the harm, if it is understood that a man like us grasps the divinity, and does not become a more God-man? We will answer that there are a thousand things that can be opposed to the contrary, and that are almost as significant as a nod, that we must constantly resist, and not believe that it is so.

Come before other things. Let us see the manner of the dispensation, which was made with the flesh, and let us scrutinize more closely the nature of our affairs. He did not know God, who is nature and truth; He worshiped the creature for God. How, then, could he be freed from such evils? Shall we say that it was right for humanity to grasp the divine nature, which did not know at all what the dignity of the heavenly nature was, since it was occupied by the darkness of ignorance and defiled by the filth of sin? How could it be possible for him to grasp the holy nature and receive glory, which no one can find unless he receives it? For let us grant that he may have known and will know how to grasp God for the Deity. Who is it that taught? For how will they believe unless they hear (Rom. 10:14)? Moreover, this is not to grasp the deity, and to take the glory that is due to him.

Therefore it is more decent, and indeed right, to feel this way, that, wishing to preserve what had perished, God came down to us the Word, through which he poured all things into himself, and into himself that which was not, so that the nature of man, that which was not, might become ; and revealing the dignities of the divine majesty through union, which is lifted up more beyond nature than the invertible God casts below nature. It was fitting that the incorruptible nature should take hold of the corruptible, in order to deliver it from corruption. It was fitting for him who did not know how to sin, to be conformed to sinners, in order to control sins: for just as wherever there is light, the darkness of darkness destroys it; so even with immortality present, every fugitive pestilence will surely depart; and when he is present to him who knows no sin (who also made his own body, which is without sin), all sin will give way.

But the fact that the Word, when he was God, became a man, and no more a man τεθεοφινός is meant Christ, can be shown even from the sacred letters. Blessed Paul therefore said of the Only Begotten: Who, being in the form of God, did not think of robbery, that he might be equal to God; but he emptied himself, taking the form of a servant, and was made in the likeness of men, and was found in the habit of a man. He humbled himself by becoming obedient to the point of death, the death of the cross. For this reason, God also exalted himself and gave him the name, which is above every name, so that at the name of Jesus Christ every knee should bow, of those in heaven, and of earth, and of hell, and that every tongue should confess that the Lord Jesus Christ is in the glory of God the Father (Phil. 2:7).

Whom, then, we shall say, is in the form of God, and in the equality of the Father, and this is not a premeditated robbery; but that he descended rather into emptiness, and into the form of a servant, and humbled himself, and was made in our likeness? If man was made of woman, naked and only: how did he have fullness, so that it is understood that he was emptied? Or is he said to have humbled himself, having previously been placed in an exalted position? Or how was he made in the likeness of men, who was that and before by nature, though he might not be said to have become that? But where is he emptied, assuming the fullness of the deity? Or how could he not become the highest, who ascended to the glory above?

Therefore, we say that man was not made God, but rather that he was made in emptiness, because of humanity, God the Word, who was in the equality of the Father and form: for he was emptied in this way, because of our likeness, when he was full, as God. He was humbled because of the flesh, so that he did not descend from the pinnacle of the divine majesty; for he has a very high seat. He was made in the likeness of men, since he is of the same form with the Father, being the image of his substance. But since he was once made near to us, he is said to have ascended with the flesh into the glory of divinity, which indeed he clearly has as his own, but he was in it in another covenant, for the sake of humanity: for he is believed to be the Lord of all, even with the flesh.

Now every knee bows to him, and that not to the pain and insult of the Father, but rather to his glory: for he rejoices and is glorified, while the Son is adored by men, although he was made like us. But it is written again: For he did not take hold of angels, but of Abraham's seed; hence he had to be likened to his brothers in all things (Heb. 2:16). Behold, the seed of Abraham took hold of the Word, God, and not a man, I do not know who has taken hold of a deity like ours, and he himself is assimilated to us, and is called our brother [Bal. omg ours], as a man, not as much as it is to the nature of the deity. For the children partook of flesh and blood, and he likewise partook of them, that by death he might destroy him that hath the dominion of death, that is, the devil, and deliver them that were bound by the fear of death throughout their whole life into slavery (Ibid. v. 14). Behold again, he, in the same way as we, partook of blood and flesh, and that thing has an immediate and proximate cause; for it is written: For it was impossible for the law, in which he was weak in the flesh, God sent his Son in the likeness of sinful flesh, and for sin condemned sin in the flesh (Rom. 3:3). Observe again that it is not man who is shown affecting the divine nature and ascending to its dignity; but rather God and the Father sent his Son, in the likeness of sinful flesh, to destroy sin. Therefore, the Word, being God, plunged himself into emptiness by becoming a man, and not simply a man, affecting the divine glory, Christ is seen.

CHAPTER XIII. That Christ Jesus is called man became God the Word. Considering more precisely the mystery of the dispensation of the incarnate only begotten, we affirm this, keeping the right and true faith: that the very Word of God the Father, true God from true God, and light from light, was incarnate, and became man, and descended, and suffered, and rose from the dead for thus the great and holy synod defined the symbol of faith.

But searching and desiring to discern what it is, finally, that the Word of God was incarnate, and made man: we see that this is not, to assume man as in conjunction, which takes place through equality of dignity, or authority, or through the sole filiation of ὁμωνυμίαν; but rather to become a man near us (in such a way, however, that no conversion or exchange follows), and to relieve him together with his nature, who was in the assumption of flesh and blood dispensationally.

There is one, then, who before the Incarnation is named by the divine Scriptures, and the Only-begotten, and the Word, and God, and the image, and the light, and the figure of the substance of the Father, and the life, and the glory, and the splendor, and the wisdom, and the power, and the magnificence. and the Lord Sabaoth, and other such names as are truly appropriate to the deity. But after the Incarnation man, Christ, Jesus, propitiatory, mediator, first fruits of those who sleep, firstborn from the dead, second Adam, head of the body of the Church, since the ancient names also follow him: for all things belong to him both in the past and in the latter times.

There is one, therefore, and who before the Incarnation was the true God, and who remained in humanity what he was, and is, and will be. Therefore, the one Lord Jesus Christ is not to be distinguished into man separately, and separately into God; but we say that Jesus Christ is one and the same, not being ignorant of the difference of natures, but keeping them unconfused among themselves.

Therefore, the sacred letter often mentions that in Christ all the fullness of the divinity dwelt bodily (Col. 2:9); We do not therefore say that God the Word dwelt separately in another Christ, in a man; nor do we further divide those things which are united, we understand two sons; but that is more, that Christ is sometimes called a sacred letter in part, and that the humanity of God's Word, which is proper to him, he has put in the place of a temple. It is also written about human souls: But they dwell in clay houses, of which we also are of the same clay (Job 4:19). Therefore, since he calls yellow houses human bodies, and affirms that souls dwell in them, shall we divide one man into two men? But it is not at all irrational that a man should be said to dwell in his own spirit. Therefore, even if the figure of prayer proceeds by means of this kind, since it cannot be done otherwise, it is not for that reason that the natures of things should be corrupted, but rather that they should be preserved according to the correct tenor of truth.

Whenever, therefore, things which are of a different nature, having been allotted to one another, are gathered together into a union, they are seen by composition; they are named by us. For it is said, as I said before, that his spirit dwells in man, and yet man is not said to have his spirit apart from his body. And the divine Paul reminds us of such a thing in an oblique sense, saying: For though our outward man is corrupted; but the interior is renewed day by day (2 Cor. 4:16). If, therefore, someone says that our inner man dwells in the outer man, he has indeed mentioned the truth, but he will not be seen to divide the one into two. And somewhere the prophet Isaiah also says: My spirit waits for you, Lord, in the night (Is. 26:9). Is his spirit said to watch for God as someone other than himself? Doesn't that seem very silly? Therefore, it is indeed necessary to know the figures of speech, yet not to depart from the competent understanding, but rather to relate the force of the sentences to the sense which suits each thing.

Although Jesus is said to be advanced in age, wisdom and grace (Luke 2:52), this is a matter of dispensation. Indeed, God allowed the Word to advance humanity in his own way, and as if he wanted to reveal the glory of his divinity little by little, and to extend it with the age of the body as well, lest something new should be seen, and that should terrify some with too much novelty. When, above all, they would also say: How does this man know letters when he has not learned them (John 7:15)? Therefore, bodily increase, and the progress of grace, and of wisdom, belong to the measure of humanity; but we confess God the Word himself, by his very nature, most perfect, not set forth in need, not of wisdom, not of grace. For he imparts wisdom, grace, and all good things to creatures.

But if Jesus is said to have suffered, it will indeed be a dispensational passion; yet it is said of him, and rightly so, because his own body suffered, and he himself was in a patient body, who could not suffer, for he is impassive, as God: yet, as far as he pertained to the insolence of the condemned, he would have suffered if he could have suffered. Therefore, since the Only Begotten was made like us, whenever a man is named by the divine Scriptures, looking at the dispensation, let us also acknowledge God himself by nature.

CHAPTER XIV. Examples of the divine Scriptures that the Word of God made man remained God. Of the propitiatory God said somewhere to the pontiff Moses: And you shall make a propitiatory chamber of pure gold, two and a half cubits long, and one and a half cubits wide: and you shall make two cherubims adorned with gold and placing them on each side. One cherub on this side, and one cherub on that side of the mercy seat. And thou shalt make two Cherubim upon the two sides. They will be Cherubim extending their wings upwards, overshadowing with their feathers over the mercy seat; and their faces looking at each other will be propitiatory (Exodus 25:17). The most certain riddle is that God the Word remained God even in humanity, and in his glory and majesty, even though because of the dispensation he was made like us: for through faith he became Emmanuel for us (Rom. 3:25). And the wisest John confirmed this to us, saying: My children, I am writing to you, that you may not sin; but if anyone sins, we have a Comforter with the Father, Jesus Christ the righteous; and he is the atonement for our sins (John 2:1). And not even Paul: Whom, he says, God set forth as propitiation through faith in his own blood (Rom. 5:25).

Moreover, see the Cherubim surrounding the mercy seat, and actually overshadowing it with feathers; but they turned to the propitiatory, and fixed their eyes on the Lord almost nodding. For the holy multitude of heavenly spirits only look to the will of God and are never satisfied with the sight of God. Thus, the prophet Isaiah says that he saw the Son, in the highest and most eminent seat, surrounded by the Seraphim and obeying him, as God (Is. 6:1).

CHAPTER XV. Another thing about the rod of Moses. The divine Moses was once destined to deliver Israel from the violence of the Egyptians. But since it was necessary to first teach those who were under the yoke of unusual servitude, that God had already reconciled to them, he commanded him to perform miracles: for usually a miracle brings us to faith. Moses therefore said to Almighty God: But if they do not believe me, and do not listen to my voice, saying: God has not appeared to you; what shall I say to them? The Lord then said: What is this that is in your hand? He answered: A rod. And he said to him: Throw her on the ground; and it became a serpent, and Moses fled from it. And the Lord said to Moses: Stretch out your hand and take hold of his tail; and stretching out his hand, he took hold of the tail, and a rod became in his hand. And he said to them: that they may believe you, because the Lord God of their fathers appeared to you, the God of Abraham, and the God of Isaac, and the God of Jacob (Ex. 4:1). Observe in these the nature and truth of the Son of God, as if he were a sort of rod of the Father; and the rod is the sign of the kingdom: for he gave the Son to have all power (John 17:2). Hence also the divine David: Your throne, God says, is forever and ever, and the rod of justice, the rod of your kingdom (Ps. 44:7). But he threw it to the earth, that is, he surrounded it with an earthly body, or sent it to the earth through humanity: for then he became in the likeness of evil men, that is, the serpent is a sign of evil.

Now we know that this is true. For our Lord Jesus Christ Himself, in image and form, because of the dispensation made with the flesh, is taken for the serpent, which Moses erected to ward off the bite of the serpent (Num. 21:8). For he said: And as Moses lifted up the serpent in the wilderness, so must the Son of man be lifted up, that all who believe in him may not perish, but have eternal life (John 3:14). For just as the serpent made of brass was the cause of salvation for those who were in danger (for those who looked to him were healed), so also the Lord Jesus Christ to those who see him indeed in the likeness of the wicked, because he became man, yet they do not know that he is the life-giving God. it will be the cause of life, and gives the ability to avoid poisonous animals, that is, contrary powers.

Let this also be a figure of this matter, that the rod of Moses devoured other rods, which the magicians had thrown to the ground (Exodus 4:2). Therefore, the rod was indeed thrown into the ground; however, it did not always remain. But it was taken up again, what it was: for although it was made, as I said before, in the similitude of our Father's rod, that is, the Son, who has power over all; nevertheless, filled with dispensation, he flew back into heaven, and was again as in the hand of the Father the rod of equity and of the kingdom: for he sits at the right hand of his parent in his own majesty, occupying the highest seats, even with the flesh (Ps. 44, 7).

CHAPTER XVI. Another thing about the hand of Moses that was leprous and completely healed. And the Lord God said to him again: Put your hand into your pocket; and he put forth his hand from his bosom, and his hand became like snow. And he said again: Put your hand into your pocket: and he put his hand into his pocket, and brought it out of his pocket, and it was again restored to the color of his flesh (Exodus 4:6). The divine Scripture names his true Son at the right hand of God and the Father. For he brought him in saying: I have established the heavens with my hand (Is. 48:13); nor even the divine David sings: By the word of the Lord the heavens are established (Ps. 32:6). See, then, that his hand was still hidden in Moses' bosom, and not yet made leprous, but when brought forth immediately became leprous; Therefore, as long as God the Word was in the bosom of the Father, he shone with the luster of divinity; but when he was in some way outside through incarnation or ἐνανθρώπησιν, he was made in the likeness of sinful flesh, and was counted among the wicked (Rom. 8:3; Is. 53:12). For the divine Paul said that he who knew no sin was sin for us, that we might become righteousness in him (1 Cor. 5:5-21). I think this means leprosy, for a leper is unclean according to the law (Lev. 13:2). But since he was once more in the bosom of the Father (he was taken up in the resurrection from the dead), his hands seemed to be stretched out clean again: for our Lord Jesus Christ will come after the times, in the sincerity of divinity and glory, although he has not cast off our likeness. For the blessed Paul also said of Christ: Because he died once to take away the sins of many. Secondly, he will appear without sin to those who wait for him for salvation (Hebrews 9:28). Therefore, whenever the sacred letter mentions Christ Jesus to us, lest you should think of man as separate, not truly united to God the Word himself; but you thought that the Word Jesus Christ, when he became man, was rather from God and the Father.

CHAPTER XVII. That Christ was not a God-bearing man, nor did God the Word simply dwell in man; but that he was made more fleshly, or a perfect man, according to the Scriptures. Let those who have an immaculate faith in Christ, and confirmed by all the right votes, say that God the Word himself descended from God the Father into emptiness, taking the form of a servant, and making his own body, which was born of a virgin. that he was made like unto us and was called the son of man. But God is indeed according to spirit; but man is the same according to the flesh. Then the divine Paul addressed the Jewish people, saying: God, who once spoke to the fathers through the prophets, will do many things and in many ways, in these last days he has spoken to us in the Son (Heb. 1:1). And in what way is it to be understood that God and the Father spoke in the last days in the Son? For he spoke to the ancients by him giving the law, and therefore the Son himself says that his words are his, spoken by the wisest Moses. For he said: Do not think that I have come to destroy the law or the prophets. I did not come to pay, but to fulfill. For I say to you, one iota or one iota will not pass from the law until all is accomplished. Heaven and earth will pass away, but my words will not pass away (Matt. 5:17). Add also the voice of the prophet: He who spoke, I am present (Is. 51:8). Therefore, when the Son became in the flesh, then the Father spoke to us in him, as the blessed Paul says, in the last days (Heb. 1:1). But let us not believe too little that he is the one who was the Son even before the ages.

Man, therefore, was truly made by him through whom God the Father made the ages; and not, as some suppose, in man, so that man is understood by us as having God indwelling. For if they really trust that they have these things right, it will be seen that the blessed evangelist John is superfluous when he says: And the Word was made flesh (John 1:14). For where is the need for human beings? Or why does he say God the Word incarnate, if he was not made flesh? The force ἐνανθρωπήσεως signifies that he was made like us, and that he remained thus also above us. nay, above the whole creation itself.

But I think it necessary, what I have said, also to confirm and convince by examples, that the Only Begotten became man, and is God, even with flesh, and not only dwelt in man, making God himself, as others who were partakers of his divinity.

CHAPTER XVIII. That Emmanuel had a different indwelling God than we do. God said somewhere about us: I will dwell among them, and I will walk in them, and I will be their God, and they will be my people (Apoc. 3:20). And not even our Lord Jesus Christ himself: Behold, I am coming; and if anyone opens the door to me, I will come in and dine with him, and the Father, and we will come to him and make our abode with him (John 14:16). We are also called the temple of God: For you, he says, are temples of the living God (1

Cor. 3:17). And again: Do you not know that your bodies are the temple of the Holy Spirit who is in you, whom you have from God (1 Cor. 6:19). But if they say so, let them openly confess that they also have Emmanuel himself, and, just as each one of us had God dwelling in him; when they see him adored, both by us and by the angels, both in heaven and on earth, let them be ashamed, as if they felt different and strange, and did not know the purpose of the sacred letters, and did not have in themselves the faith which they handed down to us, who in the beginning both saw and ministered. By word

But if they say, that therefore God is, and that God may be glorified, because the Word of God the Father so much dwelt in him; and not because he became man; they will hear from us again: If it is sufficient for those who have had God indwelling in them, that therefore they can truly be gods and be worshiped by men, surely all angels and men are gods and to be adored; for God dwells in the holy angels. We also had ourselves in us through the Holy Spirit; but this is not sufficient to show that by nature gods are to be worshiped, and those who have the Holy Spirit are to be worshipped. Therefore, it is not for this reason that God is God, and Emmanuel is to be adored, because he dwelt in him, as in a common man, and understanding separately, God the Word; but that which was made flesh, that is, man: for God remained the same, and was to be worshipped.

CHAPTER XIX. Apostolic sayings in which God is named Christ. Concerning the mystery, saying according to Christ: That, he says, was not known to the sons of men in other generations, as it has now been revealed to the holy apostles (Eph. 3:5). And: the mystery, which was hidden from ages and generations, but now it is manifest to his saints, to whom he wished to reveal the riches of the glory of this mystery among the nations, which is Christ, the hope of glory in you, whom we proclaim (Col. 1, 26). If then, he is the God-father, and not truly God, how is he the riches of the glory of the mystery, which is announced to the Gentiles? Or how is God announced at all?

CHAPTER XX. Another thing. For I want you to know what kind of concern I have for you and for those who are in Laodicea, and for those who have not seen my face in the flesh, that their hearts may be comforted, equipped in charity, and in all the riches of the fullness of the understanding, in the recognition of the mystery of God Christ (Col. 2 , 1). Behold the mystery of God, he names the mystery of Christ, and he wants some to fully understand it in recognition of him. What understanding, then, was needed for those who wished to learn the mystery of Christ, if they were to hear that God dwelt in man? But a great deal of understanding is needed, so that you may know that the Word, being God, was made a man against.

CHAPTER XXI. Another thing. For from you the word of the Lord sounded, not only in Macedonia and Achaia; but in every place your faith, which is towards God, has gone forth (1 Thess. 1:8). Behold, he mentions again that faith was made in God, when Christ also said: He who believes in me has eternal life (John 7:25). And he preaches a sermon about himself.

CHAPTER XXII. Another thing. For you yourselves know our entrance with you, since it was not in vain; but before we suffered much, and were affected with insults, as you know, in Philippi, we trusted in God to speak to you the gospel of God (1 Thess. 2:2). Behold, speaking in God, he mentioned the gospel of God; who preaches Christ to the nations.

CHAPTER XXIII. Another thing. Remember, brothers, our labor and hardship, working night and day, lest we burden any of you; we preached the Gospel of God among you (1 Thess. 2:4). And again: Therefore, we also give thanks to God without ceasing; because when you received the word from us, you received the hearing of God, not as the word of men, but as the word of God, who works in you who believed (Ibid. v. 13). Is it not evident that the Gospel of God, and the word of God mentions the preaching of Christ, since this is most evident to all: for the grace of God the Savior has appeared to all, training us to deny impiety and worldly desires, to live soberly and justly and piously, in this world, looking forward to a blessed hope , and the coming of the glory of the great God and our savior Jesus Christ (Titus 2:11). Behold God, and great, our Lord Jesus Christ is most fully named: for it is he that, awaiting the coming of glory, we should live soberly, and hasten irreproachably. But if man is godly, how can God be great? Or how blessed is hope in him? Indeed, Jeremiah is certainly true when he says: Cursed is he who puts his hope in man (Jeremiah 1:5). For God himself cannot bring about, as I said before, what it is to carry God. Finally, let them teach us, what prevents all others from being gods and worshiping those who have God in them? But God, both great and blessed, having illumination, is called Christ by the blessed Paul, who is found saying of the Jews and Emmanuel: Whose fathers, and the testament, and the promises, and from whom Christ according to the flesh, who is above all blessed for ever and ever. Amen (Rom. 4:9).

But the fact that he preached according to divine revelation becomes clear, when he himself says: Then after fourteen years I again went up to Jerusalem with Barnabas, having also taken Titus. And I went up according to the revelation and explained to them the Gospel which I preach to the Gentiles; But apart from those who seemed to be something, lest I run into emptiness, or had run (Gal. 2:1). Preaching Christ to the Gentiles as God, he names his divine mystery everywhere. He ascended by revelation to Jerusalem, and explained to those who seemed to be something, that is, to the holy apostles, or disciples, that he might not run into nothing. But when he had come down from Jerusalem, and again attended the flocks of the Gentiles, did he amend anything from the former? Did he not continue confessing Christ to God? And therefore, he writes to some: I am surprised that you are so quickly transferred from him who called you to another gospel, which is nothing else, unless there are some who disturb you and want to convert the gospel of Christ (Gal. 1:6). And he said again: But even if we or an angel from heaven had evangelized you, apart from what you received, let him be anathema. For what reason, therefore, leaving out all others, although they had an indwelling God, he only preached Jesus as God.

CHAPTER XXIV. Another thing. It is written of Christ: Now when he was in Jerusalem on the feast day, many believed in his name, seeing the signs which he did; but Jesus himself did not believe himself to them; that he himself knew all, and that it was not necessary for anyone to bear witness about man: for he himself knew what was in man (John 2:23). If man were God-bearing, how were not many deceived who believed in his name in Jerusalem? Or why does he alone know what is in a man, when especially no one else knows? For God is said to have fashioned our hearts in detail (Ps. 32:15). Or why alone forgives sins? For he said: Because the Son has power on earth to forgive sins (Matt. 9:6). Why alone, apart from others, does he sit as an assessor of God and the Father? Why do only angels obey? Why indeed he taught us to think of the common Father, who is in heaven; But was he writing him specially for himself?

But perhaps you will say that such words are to be ascribed to the indwelling Word. Was it not therefore necessary for him, according to the proper measure according to the prophets, to say himself also: These things saith the Lord. But when he wished to sanction that which was above the law, assuming the authority of a lawgiver, he said: I say to you (Matt. 5:32).

How can he say that he is free, and not subject to God? Therefore, because the Son is in truth? And if he were a man of God, would he also be a free man according to his nature? For God alone is free and free: for he alone demands, as it were, the tributes of all; and he receives religion from all as a place of debts. Although Christ is the source of the law and the prophets, he is a God-bearing man; Is it not permissible to say that the outcome of the prophetic preachings ἀνθρωπολατρίας brought us a crime?

Then the law indeed preached: Thou shalt worship the Lord thy God, and Him alone shalt thou serve (Deut. 6:13). By what learning he led us to Christ, as if to the recognition of those who were in the shadows, more important: then, refusing to worship the God of the Law and the Prophets, shall we worship a man who has an indwelling God? For where was it better to understand God? In heaven or on earth? In a seraph, or in an earthly body?

If he was a divine man, how did he partake of flesh and blood almost like us (Heb. 2:14)? For if God indwelt, this is sufficient for him to partake of flesh and blood in the same way as we do; and thus, to participate in these is the very thing that he became man: and he also dwelt in many saints; He therefore became man not once, but very often. Why, then, once at the consummation of the ages, in the destruction of sin, is he said to have appeared through his victim (Heb. 9:26)? But how do the divine Scriptures preach one coming of the Word to us, if the God-bearer was a man? If he himself became the temple of God, how is Christ also in us? Like a temple among temples? Or as God rather in the temples by the Spirit? If θεοφόρος was a man, why is it only his life-giving body? For it was necessary that the bodies of others should also be such in which the Almighty God dwelt.

And the divine Paul also wrote somewhere: Whoever makes the law of Moses angry, dies without any mercy for two or three witnesses. But the law was divine, and the commandments given by angels. How, then, will he be worthy of a worse punishment who has defiled the blood of Christ? Or how is faith in Christ superior to religion, which is according to the law? But, as we have already said before, Christ is not like the other saints, a man of God, but God more truly, and possesses a glory higher than all the world, because since God is the nature of the Word of God, he became flesh, or a perfect man: for to be animated and rational, that which is united to it, we believe the body, and the union is absolutely true.

CHAPTER XXV. How should we understand: The Word became flesh and dwelt among us; and how his proper body is called Blessed Paul mentions that Abraham's seed took hold of the only-begotten Word of God (Heb. 2:16); and not even that he partook of flesh and blood almost as we do (Ibid. 14). But we are also mindful of John; for he says: The Word was made flesh and dwelt among us (John 1:14). This, then, was the aim of spiritual men, to teach that the Word of God is tolerant of conversion; or that it is the very right to endure an exchange which is more fitting for a creature: so much so that that which was not, perhaps becomes that of its own accord; or another pushes against his will to another nature; away For he remains the same, excluding from his nature all change, not knowing to suffer the shadow of conversion: for he is always fixed in his heavenly and heavenly nature.

How, then, the Word was made flesh, it is necessary to see. In the first place, indeed, the divine Scripture generally names the flesh as man, and makes the meaning as if from the part of the whole animal; for it is written that all flesh shall see the salvation of God (Luke 3:6). And the divine Paul himself: I have not consented, he says, to flesh and blood (Gal. 1:16). Moses, the pontiff, addressed those who are from Israel: Your fathers went down into Egypt with seventy-five souls (Deut. 10:22). But it is not for this reason that you will say that naked and fleshless souls descended into Egypt; nor further that God has condescended to save his lifeless bodies and only flesh. Therefore, whenever we hear that the Word became flesh, we understand man from soul and body. Now the Word became, since he is God, a perfect man, taking an animated and rational body, and truly uniting it to himself, as he himself knows, for with our senses thoughts of this kind cannot be perceived at all, and he was called the Son of Man.

But if it is necessary to say as if looking into a mirror, human sense in some way conjectures that the Word was united to the body having a rational soul, just as man's soul is also to his own body, which is indeed of a different nature, yet a shared communion and union with the body; so that it almost seems that there is no other than the body, by the fact that by composition each animal is made one, yet remaining itself, as I mentioned before, in its own nature. Therefore it is not by exchange or conversion that we say the Word became a man of God; nor exactly that God has ceased to be; but that, taking flesh from the woman, and being united to her from the womb, man came forth at the same time as God; nor rejecting the eternal generation of God and the Father, he sustained the temporal one, taking the beginning, as it were, from the woman. But he allowed his own flesh to be born according to the laws of his own birth, for the time being. Moreover, he has in him something different from human nature: for he was born of a Virgin, and he alone has an unmarried mother; but the Evangelist mentions that he himself also became flesh and dwelt in us, in order to prove both, that he was made man, and that he did not lose his own: for he remained what he was.

For it is certainly understood that it dwells as one thing in another, that is, the divine nature in humanity, without continual mixing, or confusion, or exchange, so that it was, that which was not. For whatever is said to dwell in another, does not itself become such as that in which it dwells; but one thing is more understood in another. But truly in the nature of the Word and humanity, the only difference for us is the diversity of natures. For Christ is understood to be one of both. Therefore, without confusion, as I said before, he says that the Word dwelt in us: for he knows that the only begotten Son was made flesh and man.

But in the flesh it seems to me that the divine Evangelist wisely mentions the whole nature of men: for he says that the Word dwelt in us, and not, as I think, by the grace of another, mentioning that the incarnation of the Word took place; except that we too, being enriched by his participation through the Holy Spirit, might gain the benefit of adoption. Therefore, we believe that in Christ the highest and truest unity has been made. But if Christ is said to dwell in us, he himself will make the dwelling. But not when God is said to have dwelt in Christ: for all the fullness of the divinity dwelt in him bodily (Col. 2:9); not by shared, or simple σχέσιν, as if by the shining sun, or by sending to others the heat inherent in fire; but, so that I may say so, the divine and sincere nature itself, near all that is, making an indwelling for itself, through truth, as we said before, unity, in the temple which is born of a virgin: for thus one, and is, and is meant, Christ Jesus.

But I will not deny that our discourse is won over in the sum of expressions; but that is not why the mystery of Christ is not believed; but it should be even more wonderful with merit. For as much as he is above all in mind and speech, so much more must be placed beyond all wonder.

But we do not say that the Word made flesh, that is, a perfect man, is understood by the measure of the body, for that is most inappropriate; but in this way we also believe to fill, as usual, heaven and earth, and those things which are placed below: for all things are full to God, and all things are small to him. But how he is whole both in each individual and in all, is difficult to understand and say, nay, indeed, even impossible. But this, as I think, belongs to the fact that it is incorporeal and indivisible.

Now the proper body of the Word is called by us: not as proper is the laughter of a man, or the neighing of a horse; but that, having been made by him through a true union, should provide him with the duty of an instrument, to carry out those things which he usually does, without a single sin.

But if it may be said that God also sent the Word, lest any of you should be afraid, thinking of it, where it will go incorporeally, or where it will give way, by which all things are full? But let him know more, that there is also another mode of mission. Not that he changes place from place that is sent; but that he may undertake a more sacred service, which we learn was also enjoined upon the disciples by Christ, the Savior of all.

Finally, the divine Paul also says about Christ: Therefore, holy brothers, sharers in the heavenly calling, consider Jesus the apostle and high priest of our confession (Heb. 3:1). Note, however, that when he shows him ministering in the manner of men, although God is by nature, then he also attributes to him the office of apostleship: but, as we said before, there is nothing absurd if God is also said by the Father to send the Word; for it most assuredly fills all things, and in no place is it wholly lacking: we, however, interpreting the divine with human voices, are wont to understand the dispensation of the immortal nature by the figures of the body.

Finally, when the Holy Spirit fills everything, the blessed Paul writes and says: But because you are children, God sent the Spirit of his Son into our hearts, in which we cry: Abba Father (Gal. 4, 6). And the Savior himself said: It is expedient for you that I do it; for if I do not go away, the Paraclete will not come to you (John 16:7). It is necessary, therefore, that everything referring to the principle of piety should be followed with a certain thought: for by doing this we ourselves would benefit most.

CHAPTER XXVI. How is Θεοτόκος the Holy Virgin understood? Indeed, the Word of God and the Father was born in an inestimable way; and this generation transcends all sense and thought and is appropriate to an incorporeal nature. Nevertheless, that which is born is understood to be the proper birth of the parent, and the same substance with it. And therefore, also the son is named, namely, by the name indicating true and sincere descent; but since the Father is alive to eternity, it is necessary that he should also live to eternity, for whose sake he is the Father. Therefore, in the beginning there was the Word, and God was the Word, and the Word was also with God (John 1:1), as the wise Evangelist mentions. But in the consummation of time, for us men, he was incarnated, and man was made; not losing what he was, but retaining his unconvertible nature, and always placed in the pinnacle of divinity; receiving, however, for our sake dispensational emptiness; nor dishonoring [that is, not despising] poverty, which belongs to human nature: for when he was rich, he became poor, as it is written: that we through his poverty might be rich (2 Cor. 8:9). Therefore, man was made, and generation is said to have passed from woman. Therefore, because he received a body truly united to himself from the holy Virgin; hence we say that Θεοτόκον is the holy Virgin, because she gave birth to it humanly, or according to the flesh, although she had a generation from the Father centuries ago.

But for some to think that the Word was destined to begin from here, when man was made, is full of impiety and fury. Indeed, the Savior himself pointed out that they were most foolish, saying of himself: "Truly I say to you, before Abraham was, I am" (John 8:58). For how was it otherwise before Abraham, who was born according to the flesh after many ages? But the divine John will rebuke them enough, as I think, saying: This was he of whom I said: A man came after me, who was made before me, because he was before me (John 1:30).

Passing over, therefore, to contend in such a frivolous matter without cause, let us come rather to that which may also bring some benefit, lest some who hear it should trouble themselves that the holy Virgin Θεοτόκον is a holy Virgin, nor fill their minds with Jewish unbelief, nay, even with pagan impiety. Indeed, the Jews attacked Christ, saying: We will not stone you for a good work; but about blasphemy, that when you are a man, you make yourself God (John 10:23). But indeed, the children of the pagans mock the dogmas of the Church, hearing that God was begotten of a woman; but they will indeed eat the fruits of their madness, and they will hear from us: A fool speaks foolishly, and his heart will understand that he is vain. For the reason of our mystery, although it is a stumbling block to the Jews, but foolishness to the Gentiles; yet to us, what we know, is truly admirable, and salutary, and worthy of belief: and if there were anyone at all who dared to say that this earthly flesh was the mother of naked divinity, and that a nature superior to all creatures was born from it, that would be madness and madness . For nature was not made from the divine earth; nor will the corruptible root of incorruption ever become; nor does mortality give birth to life; nor will the tractable body become an incorporeal branch; nor shall the uncreated be born from the created; nor that without a beginning, from that which has a beginning.

But since we affirm that the Word of God was made near us, and that he took a body similar to our bodies, and most truly united it to himself, by a mysterious and ineffable reason, and thus became a man born carnally, what is absurd, or what should not be believed? Especially when the soul of man, as we have often said, is of the nature of another besides the body, yet it is born with it, when it is united to it, and no one supposes that the nature of the body provides the beginning of substance for the soul; but indeed God inestimably sends it into the body, and with it it is also born: yet we define one of the two as animals, viz., man. Therefore the Word was indeed God, but he also became man, and since he was born according to the flesh, it is necessary for humanity's sake that that which gave birth to him should be Θεοτόκος; but if the divine Scriptures do not mention God himself, she gave birth to God made man, since man could not be made otherwise than by generation from a woman. How, then, should it not be that which gave birth to him, Θεοτόκος. But we learn from the divine Scriptures that God is true, who is born from thence.

CHAPTER XXVII. Said about Christ. Behold, the Virgin shall conceive in her womb, and bear a son, and they shall call his name Emmanuel (Is. 7:14, according to Matthew and Cyril's reading). How, then, is that which was born of the holy Virgin called Emmanuel, since Emmanuel, as I said before, signifies that the Word was in our nature because of the flesh, which is the true God of the true God? But he became Emmanuel: for he emptied himself, having suffered our generation and the like, and thus conversed with us. Therefore, both God in the flesh and Θεοτόκος is truly what begat him carnally, or according to the flesh.

CHAPTER XXVIII. Another thing. For all will replace the robe gathered by deceit, and the garment with the exchange, and will, if these had been burned; for a little one was born to us, and a son was given to us, whose leadership was placed on his shoulder, and his name is called the messenger of great counsel (Isaiah 9:5, according to the LXX). You hear that a child has been named, and that a generation like ours has suffered. But heaven told him by a very bright star; the Magi worshiped those who came from the uttermost limits of the earth; The angels preached the gospel to the shepherds, saying that a Savior had been born, and announcing peace and not only the good will of the

Father: It is the message of a great plan. Indeed, he revealed to us the will of the Father, who was pleased in him to save the world (Col. 2:20), and to reconcile the world to himself through him and in him: for having been reconciled to Christ, we have been reconciled to God, for God is truly the Son of God and the Father. What therefore is the counsel of the Father, whose message was to us, he himself will teach, saying: For God so loved the world, that he gave his only begotten Son, that whosoever believeth in him should not perish, but have eternal life (John 3:16). Now the only-begotten Son is the one who was begotten of the holy Virgin: for the Word himself became man, who was God in the flesh, and thus appeared to the earthly. Finally, he said: He who believes in me has eternal life (John 6:47). But he explained that through him and in him we believe in the Father, saying: He who believes in me, but in him who sent me (John 12:44); and: He who saw him who sent me (Ibid. v. 45).

Hear me, ye islands, and pay attention, ye nations. After a long time it will stand, says the Lord; from their mother's womb they shall call my name (Isaiah 49:1, LXX). Since the Word is God, he did not ignore the fact that he would suffer generation, being made incarnate from a woman for our sake. But he knew that he would be called Christ Jesus by God and the Father; preaching to all of us the new name of his son, which is blessed on earth. Now observe that he calls his own mother, who gave birth to his body. Therefore, if she knows that she is God, she who gave birth to him carnally is called Θεοτόκος, and indeed rightly: if indeed there is no God, as some boldly, nay, rather wickedly feel, the holy Virgin herself must be deprived of this name, by which she is said to be Θεοτόκος.

CHAPTER XXIX. That God is named and man appears as the only begotten. Solomon said in prayer: And now, O Lord God of Israel, let your word be believed, which you have spoken to your son David. Is it therefore credible that God dwelt with men on earth (II Chronicles 6:17, LXX)? Observe that the incarnation of the Word is marvelous: for he dwelt with men on earth, when he was made man, for it seemed an incredible thing. Otherwise, how can that be something important, or how can that be worthy of wonder, when God does not depart from those things which he himself has created, namely, fostering them, and indeed containing those which have already been made? but creating those things which have not yet been made. But the most important miracle is that God became man and dwelt on earth with men, in accordance with the promises already given to the divine David; for it is written: The Lord David swore the truth, and it will not be thwarted (Ps. 131:11). But what did he swear? I will put the fruit of your belly on your seat. And indeed he, although he had believed that Almighty God would never deny his promise, yet he inquired more curiously about the place of generation, and therefore said: If I ascend upon the bed of my bed, if I give sleep to my eyes, or slumber to my eyelids, or rest to my times, until I find a place To the Lord, the tabernacle to the God of Jacob. Then, when he had discovered this also through the spirit, and had known the place of the carnal generation of the Only Begotten, he preached the gospel and said: We heard it in Ephrath, that is, in Bethlehem; we found her in the plains of the forest. In fact, saying Ephrath means Bethlehem, the prophet confirmed: And thou Bethlehem, the house of Ephrat (Mich. 5, 2). Now observe how Jacob, whom he believed to have been created near us in Ephrath, calls God, whose dwelling was in the tabernacle: for there the holy Virgin gave birth to Jesus.

And he mentions him and elsewhere the God of Abraham, saying: The princes of the peoples are gathered together with the God of Abraham (Ps. 46:10). For almost with the eyes of his mind, through the illumination of the Holy Spirit, educated in the knowledge of the future, the leaders of the peoples, that is, the holy apostles, saw obedience in our Lord Jesus Christ. Since, therefore, the God of Abraham and the God of Jacob, who was born of a woman, is named, why is not the holy Virgin Θεοτόκος?

CHAPTER XXX. Another thing. The prophet Habakkuk: Lord, he said, I did not hear your hearing, and I was afraid. I considered your work, and I was afraid. In the middle of the two animals you will be known: in the coming time you will be shown in it: while my soul is troubled, you will be remembered in the wrath of mercy. God will come from Theman, and the holy one from Mount Pharan (Hab. 3:1). See how he will be recognized in the middle of the two animals: for when he was born of a woman and lived until the time of the precious cross; by the grace of God, as the blessed Paul says, he tasted death for all through his body (Heb. 2:9). But since nature was God, he rose again to eternal life. He was known, therefore, who bore a precious cross for us in the midst of two animals. For he himself says somewhere to the Jews: When you have lifted up the Son of Man, then you will know that I am he (John 8:28). See also how, when naming God himself, he says that he will come from Theman, and from Mount Pharan (which is interpreted as South Theman): for Christ appeared, not from the regions of the North, but from the south of Judea, in which Bethlehem is also. When then, he who is called Lord and God, came from Judea to the south, for he was born in Bethlehem; how is not the holy Virgin Θεοτόκος?

CHAPTER XXXI. Another thing. It is written in Genesis: And Jacob was left alone, and the man wrestled with him until the morning: but he saw that he could not prevail against him, and he touched the breadth of his thigh while he wrestled with him, and said to him: Let me go, for the sun has come up. And he said: I will not let you go unless you bless me. And after another: And he blessed him there, and called the name of that place, the face of God: for, says he, I saw God face to face, and my soul was saved: and the sun rose, and the face of God passed; but he was tottering on his thigh (Gen. 32:24). The meaning of the Scriptures is indeed mystical: for it seems to indicate the struggle of the Jews, which they used with Christ, struggling almost with him; who, however, have been overcome, and they will also obtain his blessing, if they had turned to him by faith in the last times. Nevertheless, he was certainly a man who struggled, and yet Jacob called him the face of God; and not only that, but he knew that he was God according to the truth: For I saw God, he says, face to face, and my soul was saved. For God is the nature of Immanuel. It is also called the face of God. For he is the image of the substance of the Father (Heb. 1:3), and so he called himself among the Jews, when he said of God and the Father: You have not seen his face, and have not his word abiding in you, because whom he sent, you do not believe him (John 5:38).

But that God is the true man who wrestled with Jacob, the sacred letter will once again make faith; for he said: The Lord said to Jacob: Arise, go up to the place of Bethlehem, dwell there, and build there an altar to God, who appeared to you when you fled from the face of your brother Esau (Genesis 35:1). For, returning from Mesopotamia by the command of God, and fearing Esau, Jacob took the children and all his vessels.

CHAPTER XXXII. Another thing. Blessed Daniel, explaining to us a terrible vision: I saw, he said, in a vision of the night, and behold, with the clouds of heaven like a son of man coming, and he came as far as the Ancient of Days, and they brought him into his presence, and he was given honor and a kingdom: and all peoples, tribes, and languages will serve him: his power is power for eternity, which will not be transgressed, and his kingdom will not be destroyed (Dan. 7:13). You hear how no man simply remembers that he saw himself, lest one of us, and next to us, be believed to be Emmanuel; but as a son of man. For since the Word is by nature God; yet he was made in the likeness of men, and was found in the form of a man (Phil 2:7), so that both are understood in the same, that is, neither man naked, nor the Word without humanity and flesh.] he had, he mentions that it was given: for he says that all peoples, tribes, and languages will serve him. Therefore, since even the only-begotten Word of God placed in humanity has a servant creature, and the Father's principality and his own, the Holy Virgin gave birth according to the flesh herself; how is not understood Θεοτόκος?

CHAPTER XXXIII. Of the Passion of Christ; and that it is useful that according to one thing and another thing is said of one and the same thing, and we do not divide it into two. Saint Paul explains to us the salutary passion, for he says: Now the grace of God has tasted death for all (Heb. 2:9); and not also: For I delivered to you first of all that which I also received: because Christ died for our sins, according to the Scriptures: and because he was buried, and because he rose again on the third day (1 Cor. 15:3). To this also the wisest Peter: Christ says, I suffer for us in the flesh (1 Pet. 4, 1). Since then, we believe that our Lord Jesus Christ is one, that is, the sight in human form, or man-made near us, God the Word, How can we depute suffering ourselves, and yet preserve the impassive, as God?

Therefore, the passion of the dispensation was, indeed, leading to God the Word, those things which are proper to the flesh, because of the indescribable unity; but remaining outside of passion, so far as it pertains to his own nature: for God is impassive. Nor is this surprising, when we see the very soul of man, whatever the body has suffered, indeed remaining outside of suffering, so far as it pertains to nature; yet it is not to be understood that it is outside of passion, because it is his own body that suffers. And though it be unconnected, and simple; yet what is suffered is not alien. Thus, you will also understand about Christ, the Savior of all. Now I will use examples which, as if by means of an enigma, can show us that the Only Begotten indeed shared in the passion, in so far as it pertains to the familiarity of his body; but he remained unmoved by passion, like God.

And so, the almighty God commanded the wisest Moses to perform miracles, that Israel might believe him, that he had been sent by God, and that he might be delivered from violence. And he said: And you shall take water from the river and pour it on the earth, and the water you take from the river will be blood on the earth (Ex. 4:9). We say that water is indeed the figure of life, and that by nature life is the Son from the Father as proceeding from a river, according to the same substance; therefore he gives life to all things: But when you pour out water, he says, on the earth, there will be blood. When the Word became flesh from the earth, that is, when he surrounded himself with flesh from the earth, then in it he is said to have suffered a death similar to ours, although life is by nature.

CHAPTER XXXIV. Another thing. In Leviticus, God means that he is unclean and a leper (Lev. 13:1 et seq.), and thus commands that he should be expelled from the camp; and if the disease has been cured, he must be cleansed by this agreement. And taking two clean chickens, and cedar wood, and redwood, and hyssop; on him who has been cleansed from leprosy seven times, and he will be clean. He redeems us indeed, and washes away the filth of pollution, and repels the mortality of carnal concupiscence, the most precious blood of Christ, and the cleansing of the most holy baptism. Consider the rest: for, omitting to examine the power of the writings, which facilitates the mystery, we will mention it for the present. Christ is compared to two chickens, not that they are two sons, but rather that he is one of two, united in divinity and humanity. But the chickens are clean: for our God Jesus Christ did not sin; but it was the Holy Word, both in terms of divinity and humanity. But it is compared to the birds, that it is as if he were in the sublime above the earth, and from heaven above: for Christ is a man from heaven, although the holy virgin gave birth to him in flesh; in that way, therefore, from above and from heaven. For God the Word, who is from above and from the Father, taking flesh from the holy Virgin, and considering it his own, as if he had brought it down from above and from heaven, said: No one ascends into heaven, but he who descends from heaven, the Son of Man, who is in heaven (John 3:13). For those things which are his own, he always attributes to his own flesh; but once it is united, when it itself is of course valued as one.

Moreover, see that when one chicken is killed, the other is indeed washed with its blood, yet it does not die; and what is this? The Word lived, although it had died in its flesh, and it said that it was a common passion, because of the union and familiarity which it had with the flesh. Therefore, he himself indeed lives, as God; but he made the body as if it were his own, and so he took familiarly within himself the sufferings of the body, while he himself suffered nothing in his own nature. It is useful and necessary, therefore, if we accept that in one Christ that according to one thing and another is constituted of one and the same thing, and that it is not permitted to be divided into two, although they are actually said to be different from each other, and not compatible at all.

But such is what I say. We say that God the Word was born according to the flesh of a woman, although he himself gives birth to all, and calls to birth those who have not yet been born. He was born according to one thing and another, by the fact that a man like us is understood; but he calls all things to birth, because nature is God.

It is also written about him: The child prospered, and was strengthened, and was filled with wisdom and grace (Luke 2:52). Since nature is perfect, so that God, and from his fullness imparts spiritual things to the saints; since he is the giver of wisdom and grace, how does the child prosper, and be filled with wisdom and grace? According to one thing and another: for since he himself is the same man at the same time and God, indeed, because of unity, he says that he is human; but he is perfect, and is endowed with wisdom and grace, as God.

He is also the first-born and the only-begotten; But if anyone wishes to examine the actual force of the sayings, he is the first-born, who is the first-born among the most numerous brothers. but the only-begotten, as the only-begotten, is no longer the first-born, nor among many brothers. But he is himself, and this, and that; how then? According to one thing and another: for the first born, as among many brothers, because of humanity; the only begotten is the same, as the only begotten of the Father alone, and as God.

He is said to have been sanctified by the Spirit, since he is wont to sanctify those who approach; baptized according to the flesh, who baptized in the Holy Spirit How, then, does the same thing both sanctify and be sanctified; baptizes and is baptized? According to one thing and another: for man is sanctified, just as he is baptized; but he sanctifies divinely and baptizes in the Holy Spirit.

When he himself raised the dead, he rose from the dead, and since he is life by nature, he is said to be quickened, in what way? According to one thing and another: for he indeed rose from the dead and is said to be made alive according to the flesh; but he quickens and raises from the dead, as God. It is tolerated and it is not tolerated, according to one thing and another. but he remains divinely impassive, as God.

He himself worshiped with us: For you, he says, worship what you do not know; we worship what we know (John 4:22); and he is also to be adored: for to him every knee bows (Phil. 2:10). This also depends on one thing and another. For he worships, because he assumed the nature which ought to be worshiped; and the same is further adored, as if by a greater adoring nature, by that which is understood as God. But in adoration it is not to be divided into man separately, and God separately; nor, indeed, as being conjoined to God by equality of dignity, divided in substance, do we say that man is to be worshiped with him (for that is the most full of extreme impiety): but one man made to be worshiped, and the incarnate Word of God; so, however, that we may believe that the body united to it had a reasonable soul next to us. For Almighty God did not command that the two first-borns should be worshiped, both by us and by the holy angels. For there is one who was introduced into the world (Heb. 1:6); and if we examine more curiously the manner of the introduction, we shall discover the mystery of carnal dispensation. Now he was introduced into the world, when he became man, although his nature seems to be far removed from the world, and he is believed to be really in the eminence of divinity: for besides the elements, there is another creator of them. Therefore, it is according to nature that nature is God over those things which he himself created. One, however, as I said before, is to be adored, even when he was among many brothers: for then therefore he was called the first-born.

A man blind from his birth adored his only Son and was healed in a most extraordinary and wonderful manner. For when Jesus found him in the temple, he said: Do you believe in the Son of God? And he said: Who is he, Lord, that I should believe in him (John 9:38)? But Christ, showing himself to him with his body, said: And you have indeed seen him, and he who speaks with you is himself. You see that he uses a singular number, not allowing God and man to be understood separately; nay, indeed, even if he named a man Emmanuel, he by no means signified a common man; but the Word of God united to our nature. The blessed disciples adored this man as one, when they saw him walking among the waters in wonderful ways, and adored him, saying: You are truly the Son of God (Matt. 14:35).

But if we say that man is co-worshipped with God, we introduce a very wide division: for σὺν always (which is in Latin, with), unless it is posited in the signification of unity, which is by composition, completely compels two to be understood. For just as no one is said to meet with himself, nor to consort, or to worship together, or to walk together; for the preposition placed before the word introduces the signification of two persons: so even if he says that man is worshiped with God, he clearly says two sons, and separated from himself; for the reason of unity, if it is understood only in the equality of dignity, or of authority, is convinced that it is not true, and this has already been proved by many of us before.

CHAPTER XXXV. Against those who say that the only relationship between God and the Word is fitting for human beings. Some talk about the carnal dispensation of the Only Begotten, and venerable, and great, and the most lovely mystery to the heavenly spirits, by which we are also saved, bringing them to the fragile senses, they contaminate the grace and beauty of the truth; when it is necessary to try to strengthen them, not according to what seems right to them; but rather to examine, with a subtle and sharp mind's eye, the purpose of the sacred letters, and thus to enter upon the right path, following that which the most holy Fathers have examined, who, taught by the illuminations of the Holy Spirit, sanctify for us the symbol of faith, saying that God the Word was inestimably born of the substance of the Father , by which all things were made, things in heaven and things on earth; that he came down for us men, and for the sake of our salvation, became man, and suffered, ascended into heaven, and will come after the ages to judge the living and the dead.

It is true that there are some, who know that they are learned, and are opinionated, and are puffed up with brows and swellings, who, if they hear these words, laugh at them; and those things which have been so rightly said, they think more delusions: especially since we believe that the knowledge of the truth was revealed to the holy Fathers by the illumination of the Holy Spirit. But they, as if they alone could feel better things, do not think that the only-begotten Son of God, who is of his substance, God the Word suffered in his human flesh for us, although by what is meant by God, he has in his nature, so that he cannot suffer. but setting man apart and separately, who was begotten of the holy Virgin. Then, as far as it seems to them, giving him a mode of glory, they say that he was united to the Word of God the Father; and explaining the reason for the unification, they say that equality of dignity, or authority, was given by God, and that by a similar appellation, both Christ and the Son are called, and the Lord. But even if man is said to have suffered something, which is invented by them, they say that it is necessary to refer to God the Word himself, because it is joined to him by the equality of dignity, since, divided by nature, each one is what he is.

Now I will explain the force of the sentences, as much as I myself value them, setting forth examples of sacred literature. Christ was hungry, he was tired from the journey, he slept, he entered the boat, he was beaten by the officers with whips, he was flogged by Pilate, he received the spittle of the soldiers, who, piercing his side with lances, offered vinegar mixed with skin to his mouth; but he also tasted death, suffered the cross, and other abuses of the Jews. They mention that all these things indeed happened to man; but to be referred to the person of the Son of truth. But we believe, as in one God the Father, omnipotent, maker of all things visible and invisible: so also in one Lord Jesus Christ, his Son. But we refuse to divide the man Emmanuel separately, and the Word separately. But knowing that the Word became a man near us, we truly say that he is God from God; but the human man next to us is from the woman. And we further affirm, on account of familiarity, that indeed he was afflicted with infirmities of the flesh; indeed, that he preserved the impassibility of his nature, by the fact that he was not only man, but also the same God by nature; and just as his own body was his own, so also were his natural bodily and blameless passions, as well as those which were brought upon him by the mischief of some.

But he suffered impassively, because he did not humble himself for that reason, that he might be so much like us; but because, as I said before, he reserved that of his nature, that he should be superior to all. But if we were to say that through the conversion or exchange of his nature he passed into the nature of the flesh, it would be necessary for us to confess by all means, even unwillingly, that the divine and mysterious nature was susceptible. But if, although he was made man next to us, he remained unchanged, for it is proper to the heavenly nature that he cannot suffer; then, by the union of him, the body was made susceptible; but he himself remains impassive, because it is his own that he cannot suffer.

But if Emmanuel was glorified through suffering, as he himself said, when he was about to suffer a precious cross for us: Now is the Son of man glorified (John 31:31); why, when they give the glory of passion to a man who has only conjunction with him in equality of dignity, are they not ashamed? For, as they think, according to the will of the Father, He united to Himself a man who was pleased and pleased, and made him equal to His glory, and granted that by the same appellation Christ, and Son, and God, and Lord should be called.

Therefore, the Word was not truly incarnate, nor was man fully made. Is it possible that even the holy teachers of the whole world say falsehoods and lies? For they should either say, or rather proceed to the middle of proving that the mode of conjunction introduced by them has the power of incarnation, and that is, that the Word was made man. Or if they do not think that they have it so, why do they invent a method of conjunction for us that is not conjoined, disregarding the truth? when it is fitting to say of them, that the Word of God and the Father was united to our humanity: for in this way human suffering is to be understood as proper to the flesh. But in so far as it pertains to the nature of divinity, everyone is free from trouble, as God is.

But by mentioning the relation, which I do not know how they discovered, they detract from the glory of Emmanuel; and that they hardly make him one of the holy prophets; and that they constitute among the measures of the many, and are taken in it without any doubt, I will prove further, by setting forth examples from the divine Scriptures.

The people of Israel murmured at one time in the desert against Moses and Aaron, saying: Would that we had died, smitten by the Lord in Egypt, when we sat at the pots of meat and ate until we were satisfied (Ex. 16:3). Then says the wisest Moses (for it was the result of the impatience being so rashly refuted): But what are we? For your murmuring is not against us, but against God. For during those times, even Almighty God reigned, through the holy prophets, in the people of Israel.

But the Jews, also in this respect, were small-minded, and approached the divine Samuel, saying: Behold, you have grown old, and your children do not walk in your ways, and now set up a king over us who will judge us, as the rest of the nations have (1 Kings 8:5). Unfortunately, the prophet bore this too much. And the Almighty God said: Hear the voice of the people, as it has spoken to you; because they have not despised you, but they have despised me, that I should not reign over them.

But somewhere Christ also said to the holy apostles: He who welcomes you welcomes me (Luke 9:48). He also promises to address the merciful on behalf of his tribunal: Come, blessed of my Father, receive the kingdom prepared for you from the foundation of the world (Matt. 25:34). But familiarly acknowledging their honesty in regard to those to whom they had well consulted: As long as you did it, he says, to one of the least of these, you did it to me.

Behold, in these the manner of the relation is clearly known. The people of Israel murmured against Moses and Aaron, and the matter indeed had a relation to God; yet Moses and Aaron were men like us. You will understand the same agreement also in the others, of whom we have just mentioned: but they were indeed, as I said before, holy and admirable men, yet men like ourselves. In that way, therefore, even a man united to God the Word, as they say, has a relation to that of his passions? And how is it that man is no longer common, and separate, and nothing else? Therefore, God is not truly Emmanuel, not the only begotten son, not God by nature.

Then why is it that none of the others have been honored by the Word of God with equality of dignity or authority? But they contend that only this pair was the lot; especially since God is the savior of all, he does not judge in person, but just judgment, as he mentions. Why then does he sit alone? How will the judge come, obeying the angels? But why alone is he worshiped both by us and by the spirits above? But very much, says he: for we find you also doing this; for you confess the suffering itself, inasmuch as you attribute to it the passions of the flesh, although you worship the impassible as God. But we, man, when we first united the Word and man, we indeed give passions to the flesh, but we keep the impassible as God. For although he was made like us, yet we must know the majesty of his heavenly dignities and divine eminence.

We confess, therefore, that this presupposed unity, as if some foundation of faith had been laid, has been suffered in the flesh; that he remained without sufferings, since he has it in himself, so that he cannot suffer; unless, indeed, we put God and man on one side, dividing the natures from themselves, and according to the only relation we say that his Word brought about those things which happened to the body, that is to say, it has the manner of Moses and Aaron he who is born of the holy Virgin Emmanuel, which is interpreted, God with us.

Therefore, even if he says through the holy prophets: I laid my back in scourges; and my cheeks into the palms of my hands; But my face was not turned away from the confusion of spitting (Isaiah 15:6). Furthermore: They have covered my hands and my feet; they have numbered all my bones (Ps. 21:18). And further: They gave me hyssop for my food, and vinegar for my thirst. We attribute all these things to the Only Begotten, who suffered for us in the flesh as a dispensation, according to the Scriptures: For by his hand, we are healed, and he was made weak because of our sins (Ps. 68:22). But we know that he is impassive by nature: for if, as I said a while ago, man and God are one and the same, the passions of his humanity are certainly God's own, so that impassive is understood.

Feeling these things in this way, we will preserve piety, and going through right thoughts and senses, we will reach the palm of the heavenly calling in

Christ, through whom, and with whom, glory to God and the Father with the Holy Spirit forever and ever. Amen.

The Scriptorium Project is the work of a small group of lay people of various apostolic churches who are interested in the preservation, transmission, and translation of the works of the early and medieval church. Our efforts are to make the works of the church fathers accessible to anyone who might have an interest in Christian antiquities and the theological, philosophical, and moral writings that have become the bedrock of Western Civilization.

To-date, our releases have pulled from the Greek, Syriac, Georgian, Latin, Celtic, Ethiopian, and Coptic traditions of Christianity, and have been pulled from sundry local traditions and languages.

www.ingramcontent.com/pod-product-compliance
Lightning Source LLC
LaVergne TN
LVHW061042070526
838201LV00073B/5152